KBB MINI GUIDES 2016

BEDROOM PLANNING & DESIGN

Brian Rider

1

BEDROOM PLANNING & DESIGN

Please note that a few topics were covered in our previous en suite guide, but, essentially this is an original study of bedroom planning and design.

Bedroom Planning & Design

Bedroom Planning

Although we have been involved with bedroom design for 30 years this is the first on line training guide

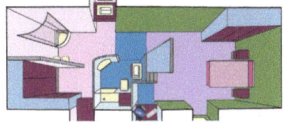

BEDROOM SUPPLEMENT

Most KBB planners and designers will at some point work on bedrooms. In many respects bedrooms have not really progressed all that much since our early days of Bernstein bedrooms and our Hammonds and Sharps course and our dedicated Planit computer course for Strachan. We have studied the market and suggested a few ideas to make an improvement in planning and design.

We have suggested in our checklist some of the things that you may wish to concentrate on when planning a luxury bedroom. This may be a bit too much for the average 3 bed semi but the 4 bed executive youngish family who enjoy life to the fullest will certainly benefit from some of these ideas. The bedroom needs to be interesting but must also suit the purpose, targeting specifically, the lifestyle and aspirations of the buyers.

Clothes

but maybe not outside clothes

It takes a bit of
imagination to create
an inspired bedroom
setting. Match the
room wisely to the
customer' needs.

Intimate wear

Fun night wear

Media centre

Ladies toys

Kindle or ipad

Charging centers for the above

Headphones and pillow speakers for audiobooks

dressing room

ensuite

lingerie & underwear

shoes & bags

dressing table - jewellery & makeup

internal storage

Interiors are crucial to the success of the project.

Only use the classic, heavy overbed storage designs so commonly used, if it is absolutely essential

pay special attention to bedside cabinet and niche detail

and especially dressing table design and function

Critique

Critique

We are going to take a look at a number of bedrooms to see how they stack up with the modern concept of a luxury bedroom.

I think you will be surprised at how mundane many of these presentations are and how much many of the current bedroom designs use only the classic feature of overbed storage.

The above plan provides a nice niche area but a very boring overbed facility.

A little more imagination could produce something far better. Have a look at the next two designs

MUCH MORE FRIENDLY LOOK - GLAZED DOORS WORK WELL

ATTRACTIVE AND EFFICIENT DESIGN WITH A TOUCH OF STYLE

2
GOOD DESIGN

Most bedroom planning is using cliches and not striving for original and well matched thinking. Need to try harder

WHAT IS GOOD DESIGN

- efficient and yet attractive use of the features available in your product range

- innovative use of the features

- style in keeping with the property

- style in keeping with the buyer's lifestyle

I find it quite strange that so many bedrooms do not have an adequate dressing table with proper facilities and a decent mirror with good lighting.

Is it all that difficult?

The following bedrooms have touches of good design but a little incomplete

3
Bedside Cabinets and Features

Although the design below has some merits it certainly cannot be praised for its lighting and other electrics.?

- Display
- lighting
- electrics for charging stations
- perhaps a charging dock
- shelving and/or niche

- drawer space
- intimate items
- medicines
- headphones for tablet and TV jac

4

Internal storage

Certainly a good volume of storage but is there enough variety?

1.drawers

2.specialist drawers for ties, belts, etc

3.adjustable hanging systems

4.multi layer hanging with drop down facility

5.shelving for shoes

6.shelving for bags

7.his and hers facilities

5

A little funky but a nice dressing table although perhaps not enough room in front of the mirror?

Dressing Tables

1.large mirror

2.multi view mirrors

3.natural lighting

4.also good overall lighting

5.theatre style lighting?

6.storage for jewellery

7.makeup

8.diary

9.tablet

10.electrics

11.chair not stool

6

ONE FOR THE KIDS

Some of these kids rooms are very comfortable livingwise but not very comfortable sleep wise?

7

Dressing Rooms

Remember, a dressing room should be designed to be a comfortable area where you can ponder your wardrobe and dress.

The key drive to a dressing room is storage, storage, storage and a well designed dressing table with real make-up facilities. Ideally a dressing room should be near an en suite and even more ideally a dressing room should act as a fully fledged closet.

8

MEDIA

In the bedroom of a modern family surely a n integral part of a media centre must be a computer?

A media centre in a master bedroom has got to be one of the must have features of any modern family . But what format should that take and what content? Only the buyer can provide that information but will they always know? Playing games in the bedroom appeals to most red blooded couples but what about playing electronic games? It may be best if these were banned

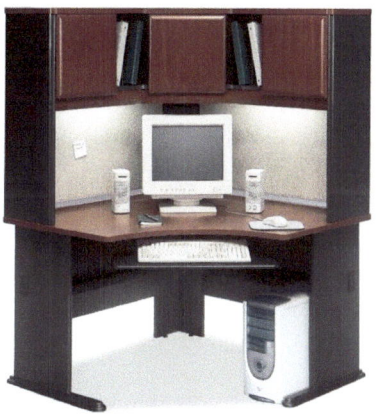

9

Dressing Rooms 2

Plenty of storage for all requirements. Often referred to as a closet or walk in closet, but there should be a distinction. Should be adjacent to the en suite and ideally, his 'n hers.

It doesn't have to be large but it should be big enough to incorporate a dressing table with a generous size mirror and good overall lighting plus a full length mirror able to easily see the view from behind and probably, ideally a chevalier mirror.

In the grander households it could be possible to have a his 'n hers dressing room and en suite for really comprehensive facilities. The his group can be smaller and would only need a shower.

Let's have a look at some plan

1

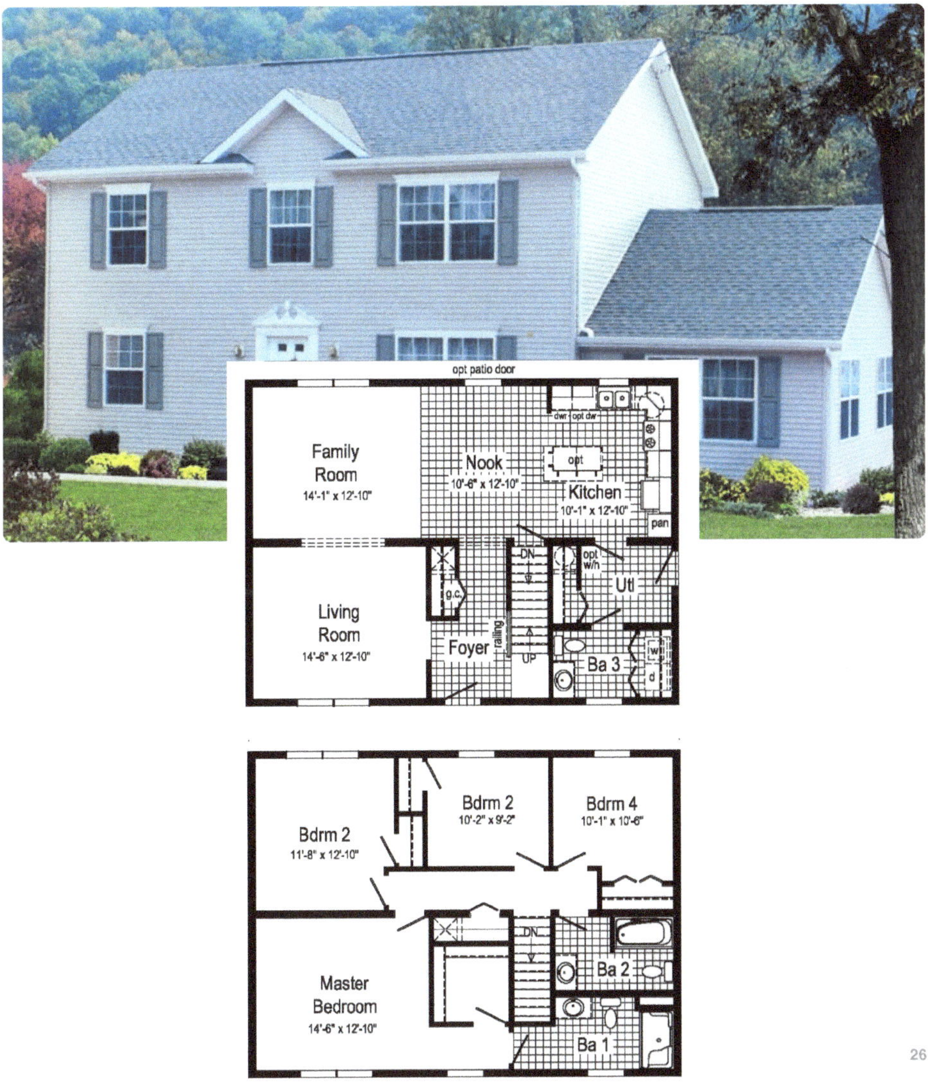

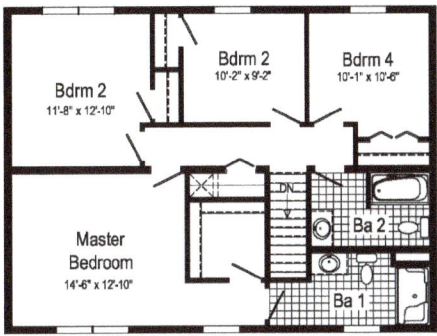

opt patio door

Family Room
14'-1" x 12'-10"

Nook
10'-6" x 12'-10"

Kitchen
10'-1" x 12'-10"

pan

dwr | opt dw

opt

Living Room
14'-6" x 12'-10"

Foyer

g.c.

DN

opt w/h

Utl

UP

Ba 3

railing

w/h

d

Bdrm 2
11'-8" x 12'-10"

Bdrm 2
10'-2" x 9'-2"

Bdrm 4
10'-1" x 10'-6"

Master Bedroom
14'-6" x 12'-10"

DN

Ba 2

Ba 1

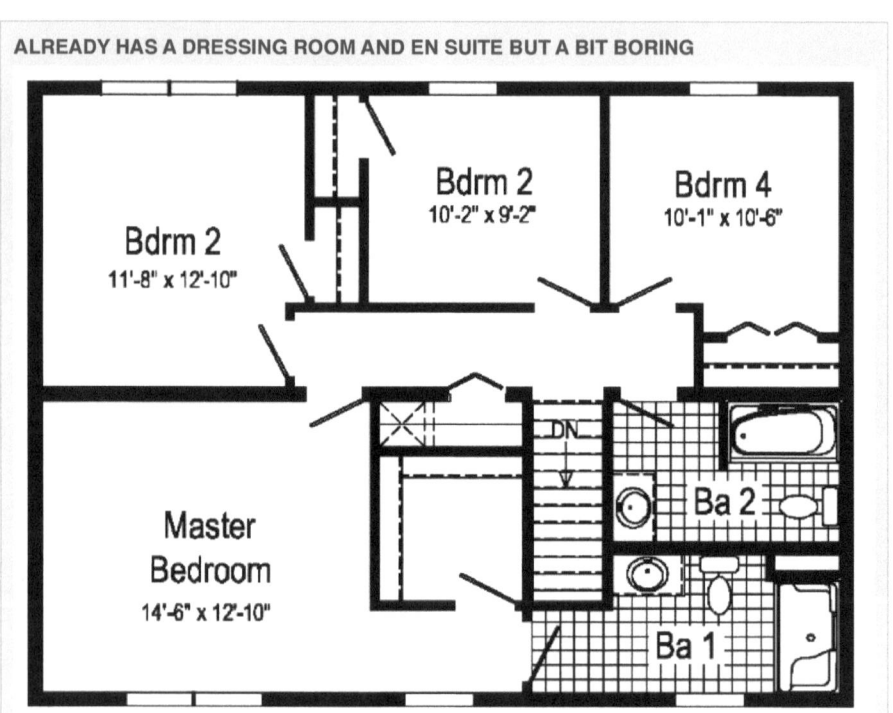

ALREADY HAS A DRESSING ROOM AND EN SUITE BUT A BIT BORING

Bdrm 2
10'-2" x 9'-2"

Bdrm 4
10'-1" x 10'-6"

Bdrm 2
11'-8" x 12'-10"

Master
Bedroom
14'-6" x 12'-10"

DN

Ba 2

Ba 1

THE CLOSET / AIRING CUPBOARD ON THE LANDING MAY BE USEFUL.

Use this as an exercise and create a more imaginative layout.

HOUSE PROJECT 2

KITCHEN
16'-0" x 9'-1"

BREAKFAST NOOK
14'-6" x 13'-0"

SUNROOM
11' 5" x 9' 3"

LIVING
14'-4" x 26'-6"

FAMILY
12'-5" x 11'-10"

DINING
16' 7" x 13' 3"

ENTRY
12'-8" x 13'-3"

OPTIONAL PORCH

MASTER BATH
10'-6" x 9'-11"

BEDROOM 2
10'-11" x 12'-8"

BATH
8'-8" x 9' 10"

UTILITY
8' 10" x 6' 2"

BEDROOM 3
12'-2" x 12'-8"

HIS & HERS CLOSET
10'-6" x 11'-5"

BEDROOM 1
16'-7" x 13'-2"

BEDROOM 4
12'-0" x 13'-2"

GENEROUS SIZE HOUSE

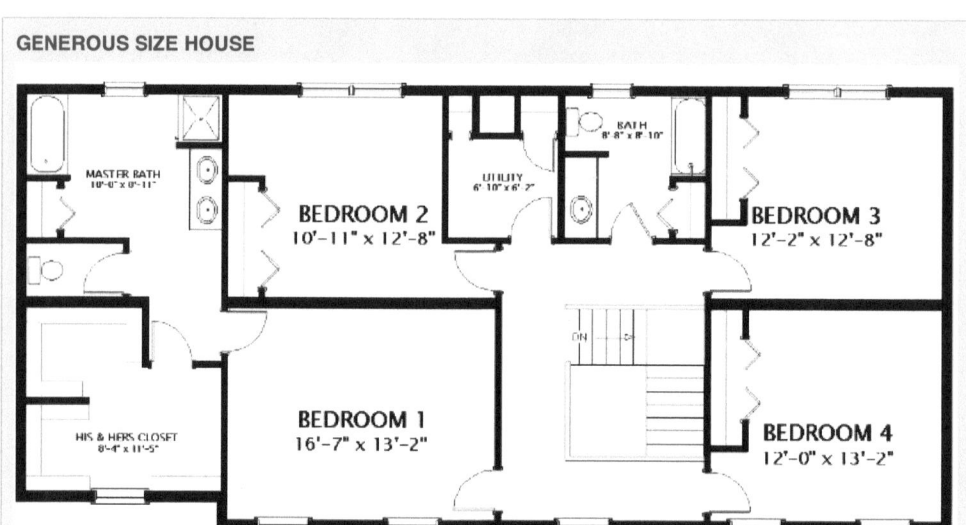

BEDROOM ONE HAS EN SUITE AND HIS 'N HERS CLOSETS - HER CLOSET IS GENEROUS SIZED FOR ALL FEATURES - BED 2 COULD BECOME HIS EN SUITE

Why is there a utility room on the upper floor? Surely this would be a better layout with a rethink on the entire layout. And why the old fashioned separate toilet. Has nobody thought of hygiene? The layout can be preserved with just a modesty panel but the small closet needs to be ditched.

USE THIS AS AN EXERCISE TO MAKE A HUGE IMPROVEMENT TO A NICE LARGE PROPERTY.

House project 3

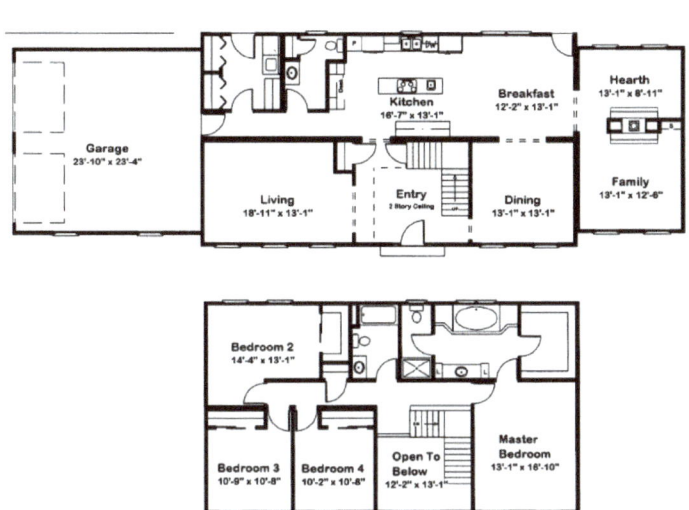

GENEROUS SIZED MASTER BEDROOM EN SUITE AND CLOSET

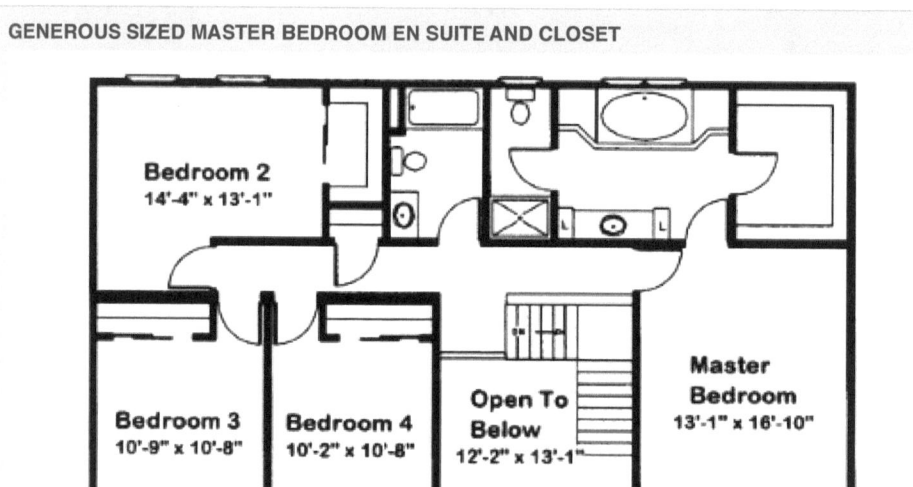

VERY LITTLE LITTLE SCOPE TO EXTEND TO HIS 'N HERS BUT THERE ARE CERTAINLY SOME POOR DESIGN ELEMENTS

Again the silly outdated separate toilet? If you cannot wash your hands you are not clean and you will contaminate door handles etc. as you make your way to the sink. THINK, THINK.

It may be nice to have an open staircase but this space could be used in connection with the master bedroom to produce a useful area, perhaps a second closet? If you are going that route it would be possible to use Bedroom 4 with the master suite and/or Bedroom 2.

If you expand your thinking in these directions I am sure you could come up with a really superior layout and one which would command a premium price.

Developing this property

This is a major project and one which requires a little more study and concentration. There is already plenty of space, but it hasn't been used all that intelligently and certainly does not provide the sort of facilities that a modern, obviously wealthy family, would like to enjoy.

For a start I would like to see something a bit more ambitious on the porch. Perhaps one of these new covered garden style glazed areas?

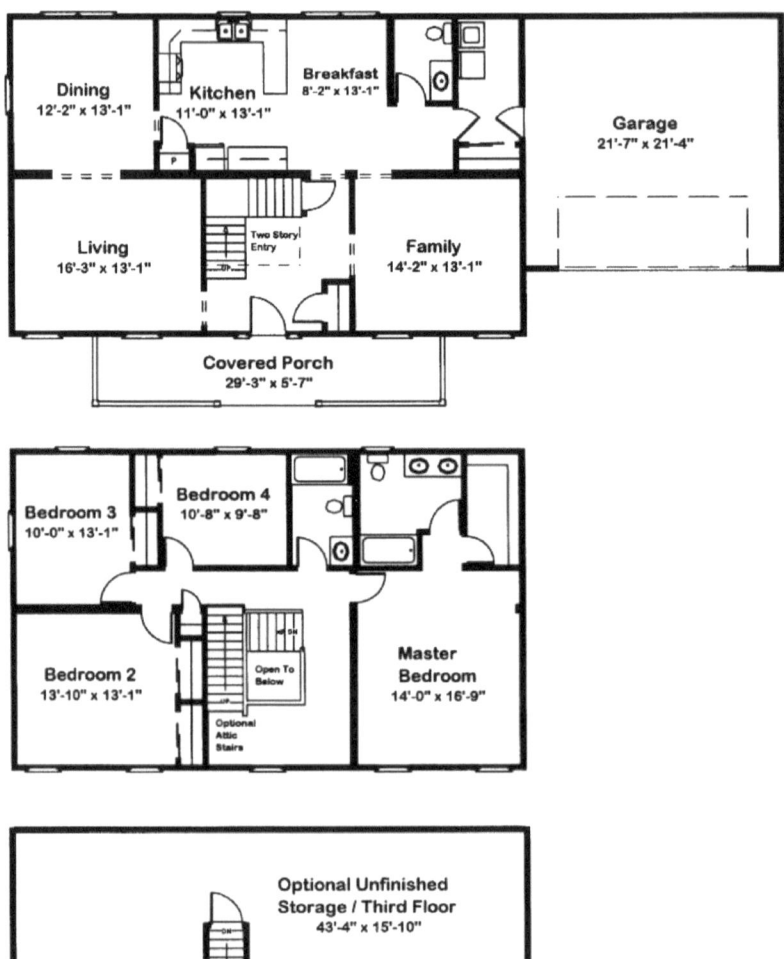

Dining
12'-2" x 13'-1"

Kitchen
11'-0" x 13'-1"

Breakfast
8'-2" x 13'-1"

Garage
21'-7" x 21'-4"

Living
16'-3" x 13'-1"

Two Story Entry

Family
14'-2" x 13'-1"

Covered Porch
29'-3" x 5'-7"

Bedroom 3
10'-0" x 13'-1"

Bedroom 4
10'-8" x 9'-8"

Bedroom 2
13'-10" x 13'-1"

Open To Below

Optional Attic Stairs

Master Bedroom
14'-0" x 16'-9"

Optional Unfinished Storage / Third Floor
43'-4" x 15'-10"

Bedroom 3
10'-0" x 13'-1"

Bedroom 4
10'-8" x 9'-8"

Bedroom 2
13'-10" x 13'-1"

Open To
Below

DN

UP

Optional
Attic
Stairs

**Master
Bedroom**
14'-0" x 16'-9"

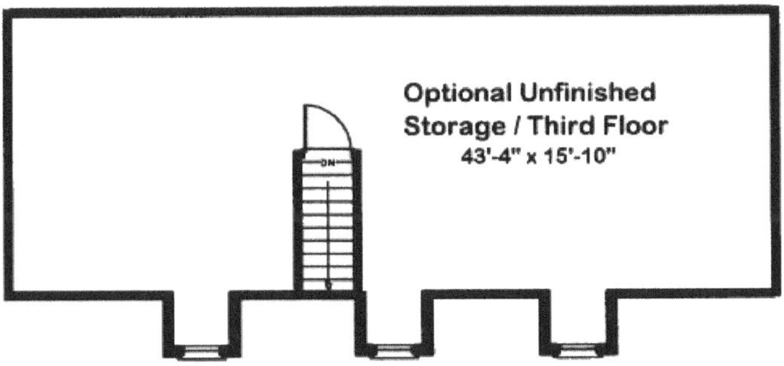

**Optional Unfinished
Storage / Third Floor**
43'-4" x 15'-10"

DN

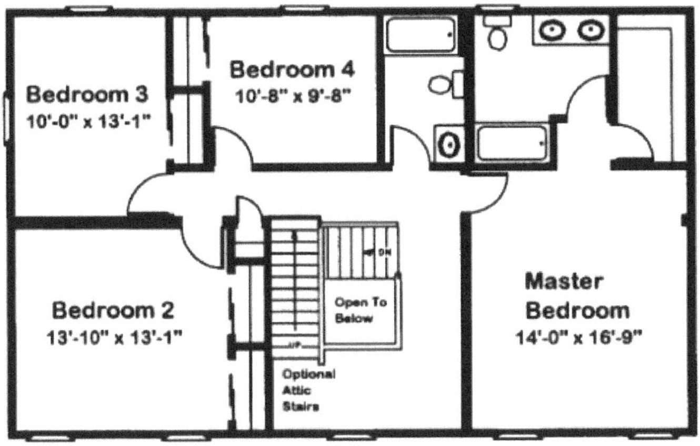

I would hate to see that top floor go to waste.

There is a lot of room going begging.

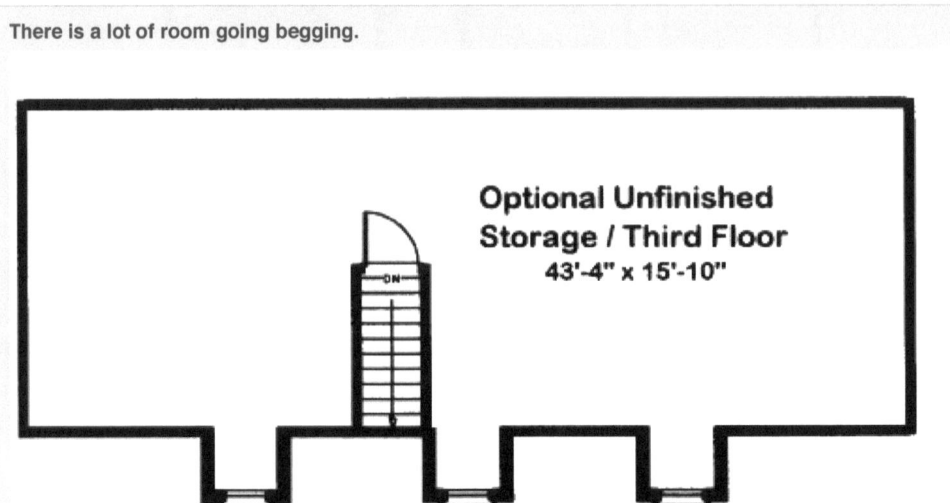

**Optional Unfinished
Storage / Third Floor**
43'-4" x 15'-10"

Nice window layout but why no windows to the rear?

There must also be a case for modifying the rear roof arrangement to provide more internal space and headroom.

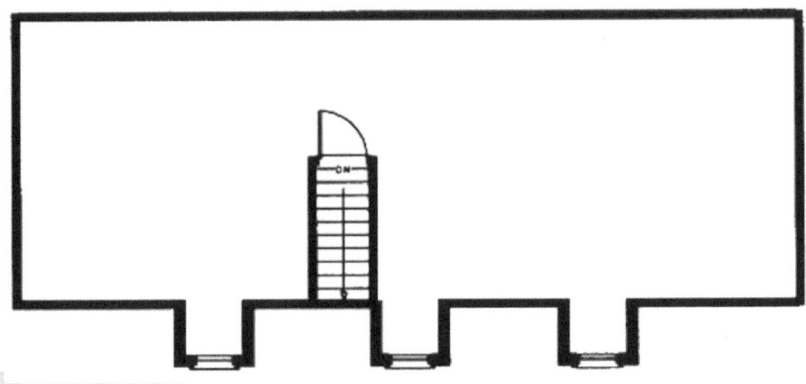

Developing this property

🌀House not built yet

🌀Third floor could be developed

🌀Stairs could be repositioned even a lift could be installed but an emergency staircase would be needed but this could go at the ends of the building

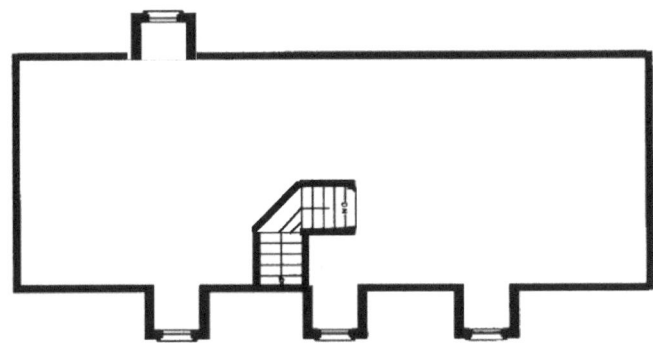

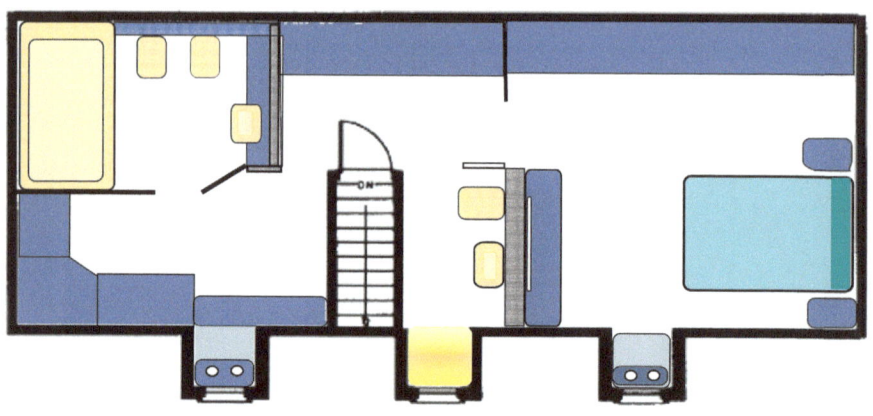

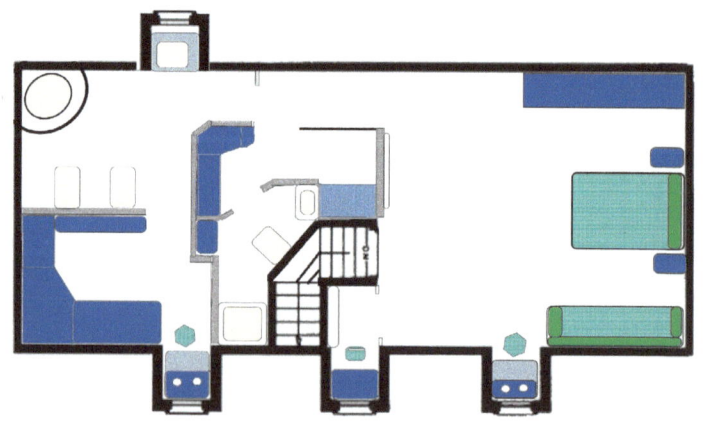

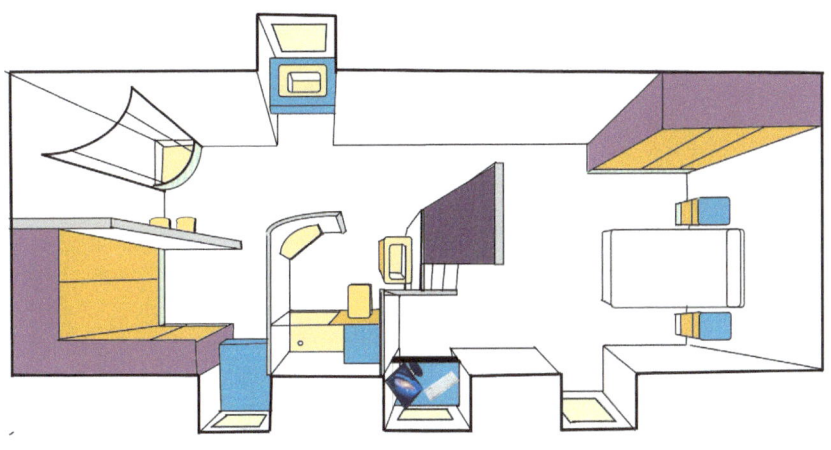

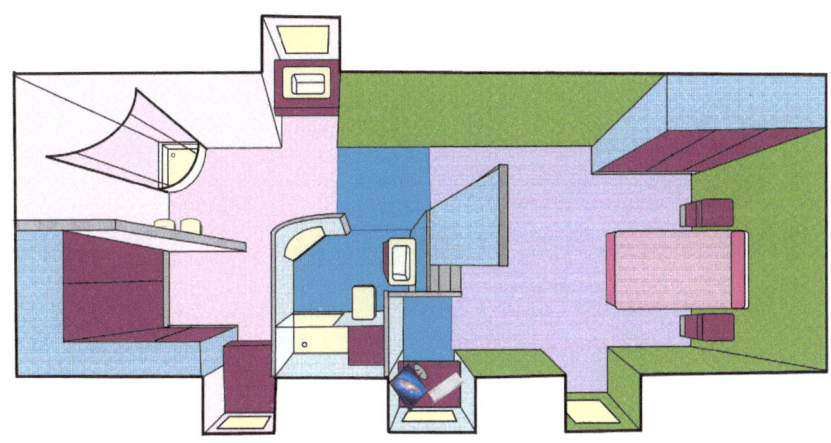

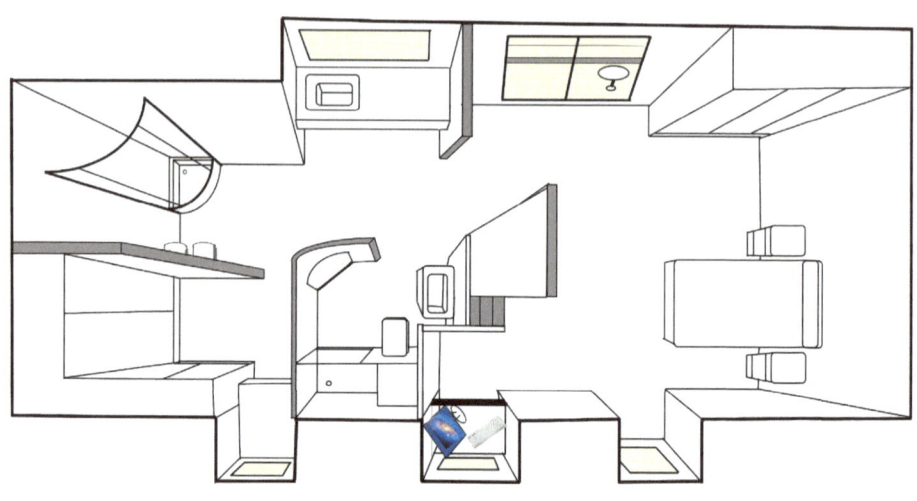

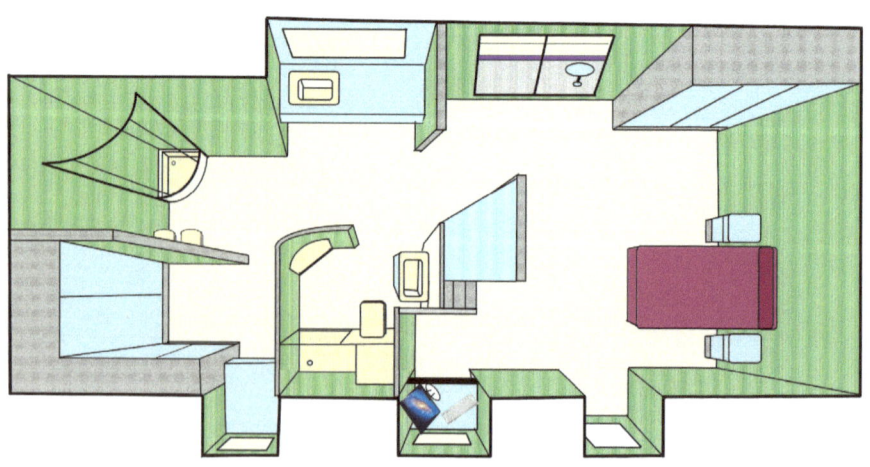

10

BEDROOM Presentation

For the first time ever, we are presenting a number of bedroom design studies and the way to most effectively present and successfully sell this sort of project: All the work has been done with Adobe Illustrator and Graphic Converter on a Mac. All within set time limits.

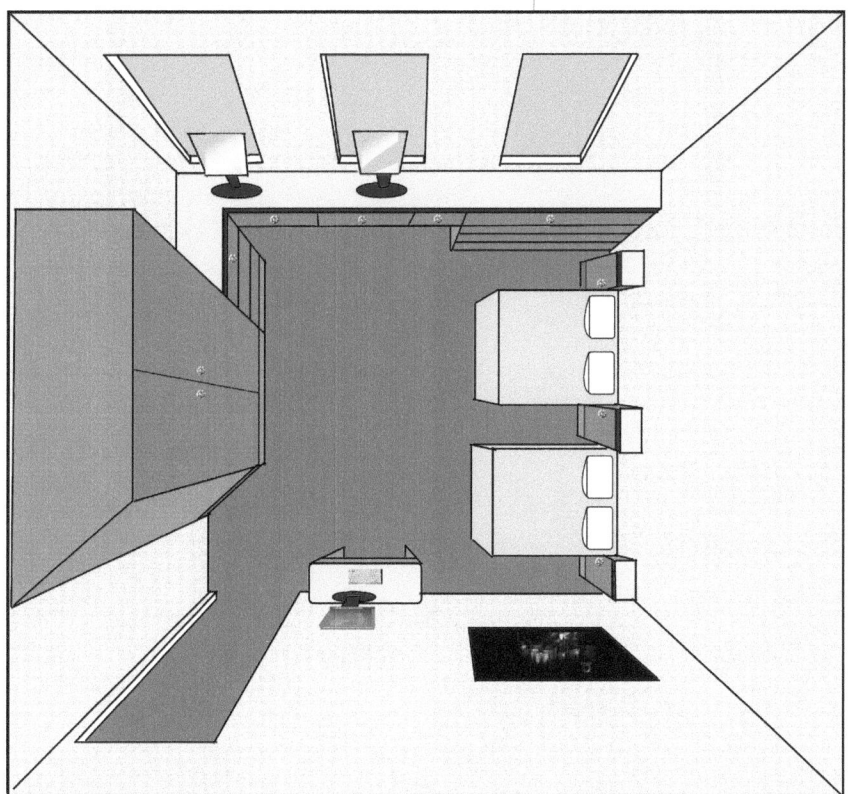

Some people have a natural talent for drawing and find it a great therapeutic pastime. Others want a good presentation in the quickest possible time and probably, like myself do not have great hand drawing skills. Using Adobe illustrator and perhaps Graphic Converter, anyone can achieve these results in a reasonable time frame.

BEDROOM STUDY A - BIRD'S EYE PRESENTATION

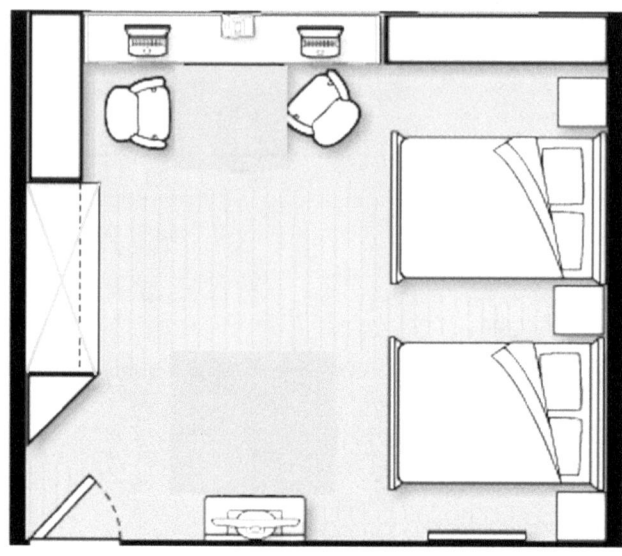

- Large Room

- all four walls with content

- cannot present with conventional 3d techniques without losing at least one wall

- robe area

- twin kingsize beds with triple bedside cabinets

- his and hers dressing table

- computer station

- av centre

- extensive drawer storage

- separate large closet so minimal robe storage

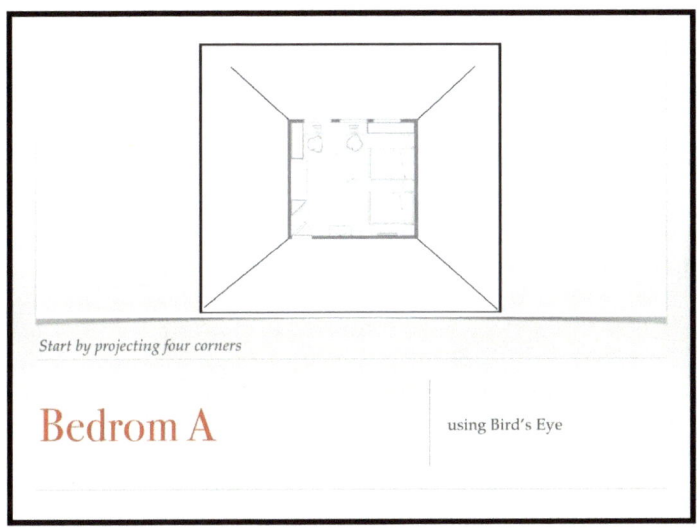

Start by projecting four corners

Bedrom A

using Bird's Eye

Birds Eye Bedroom A

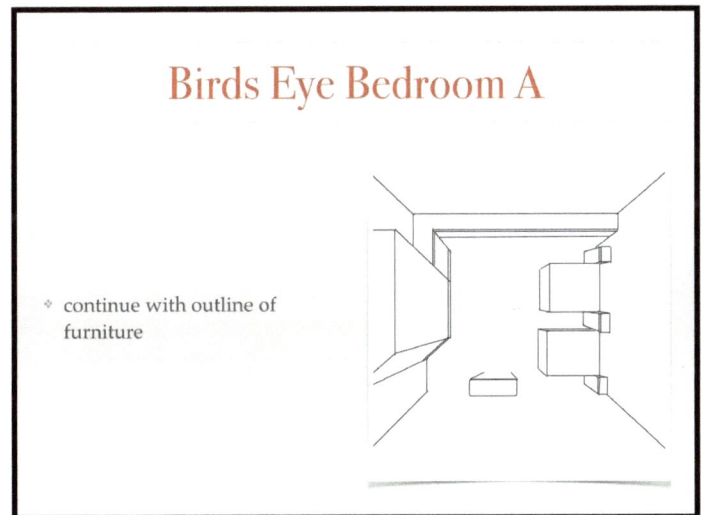

❖ continue with outline of furniture

ADD DETAIL

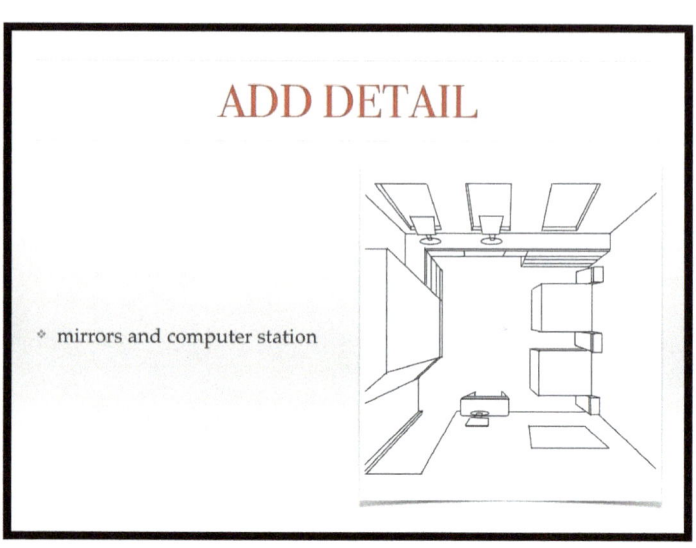

❖ mirrors and computer station

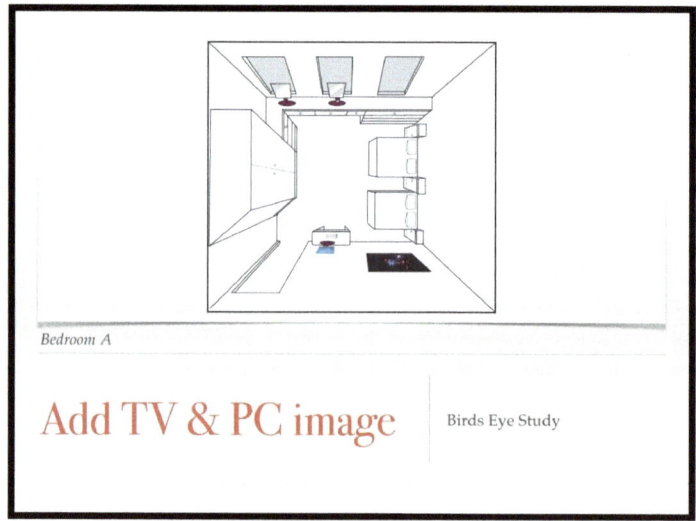

Bedroom A

Add TV & PC image

Birds Eye Study

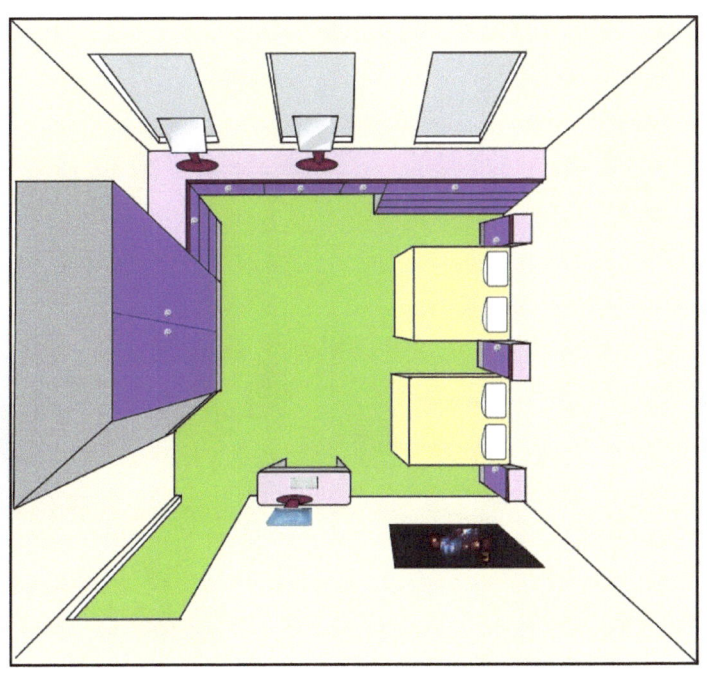

Bedroom B

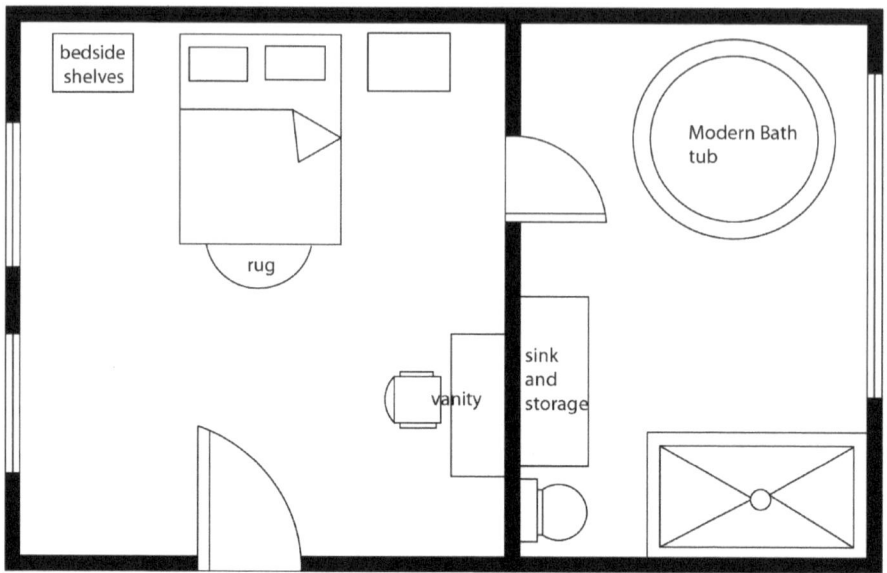

Large room but simple layout.

We are also designing the en suite so the presentation must encompass both rooms and should easily depict the entire space.

Clearly conventional presentations methods would not suffice so we have opted for an Isometric Projection which is simply an extension of the normal Isometric method.

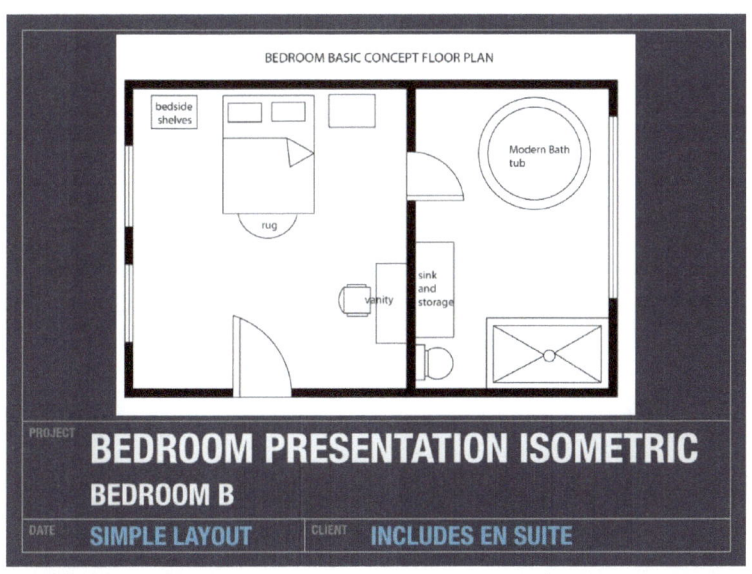

BEDROOM BASIC CONCEPT FLOOR PLAN

bedside shelves

rug

Modern Bath tub

sink and storage

vanity

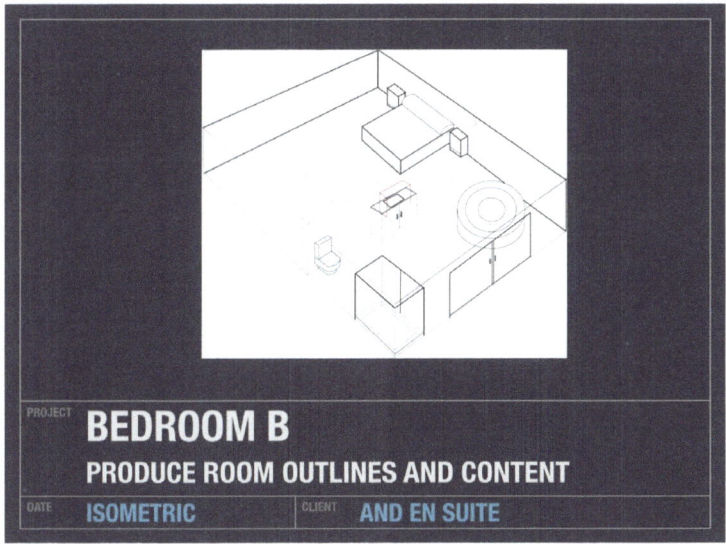

ISOMETRIC BEDROOM

- note back to back units shown in colour to identify

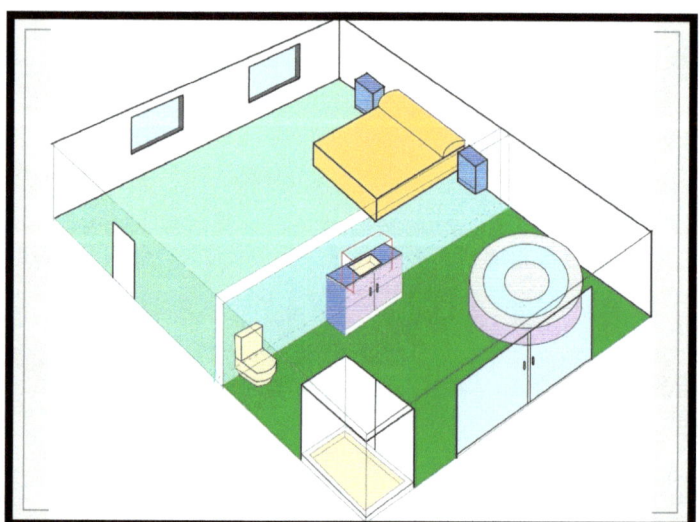

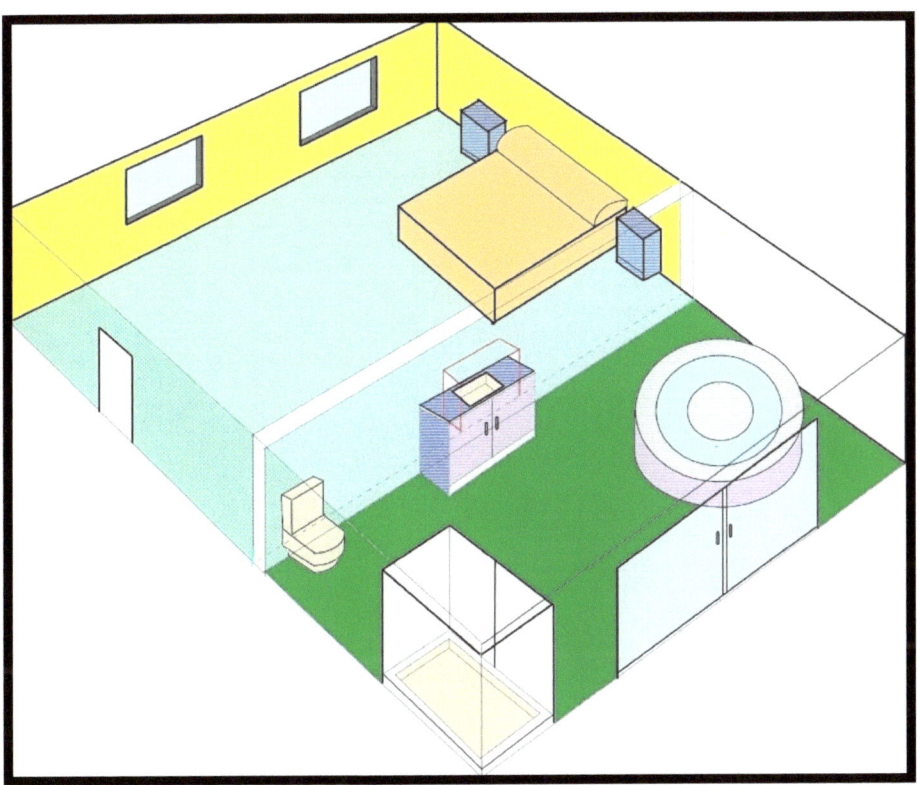

bedroom c

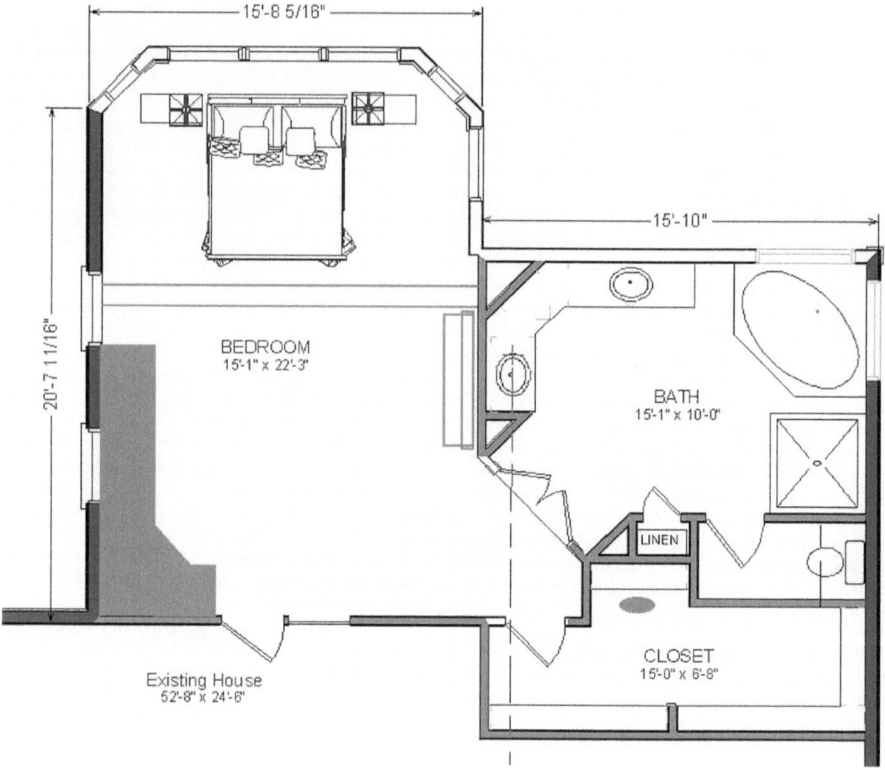

Large complex project with 3 distinct areas requiring careful and imaginative planning and presentation. this is one that will require the highest level of expertise to plan, design and present. And could also be a major challenge in execution. Clearly the designs will depend on the expertise of the installation team. Plus the consideration must always depend upon whether installation is in house or third party of even DIY. In the extreme cases your design may need to be imaginative and yet simple to execute.

This is an Axonometric study.

3 DISTINCT AREAS

BEDROOM C

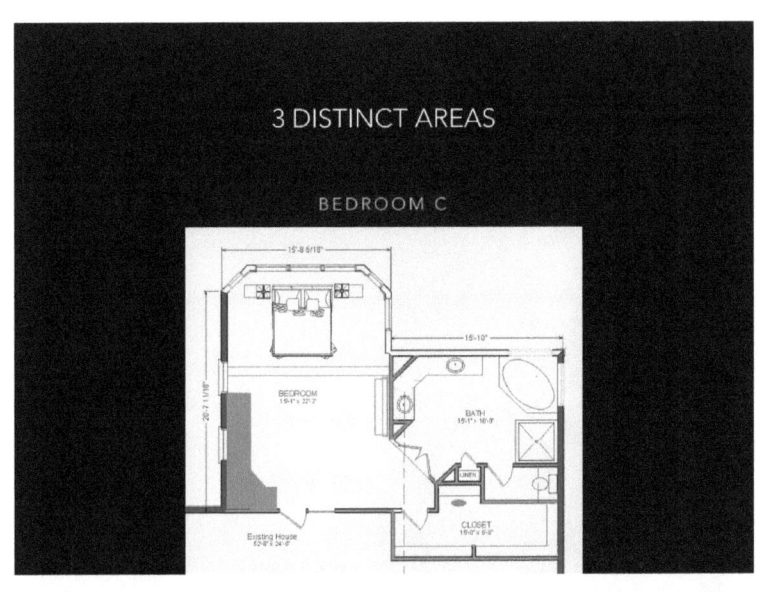

BEDROOM C

- configure basic room outline

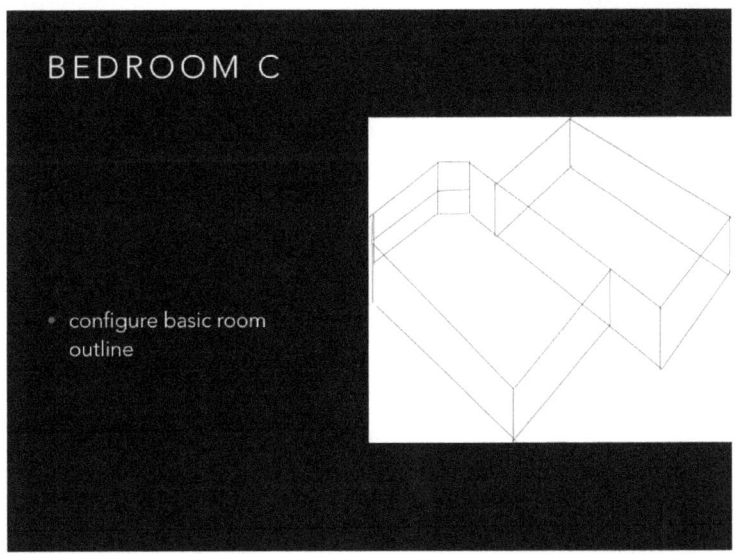

BEDROOM C

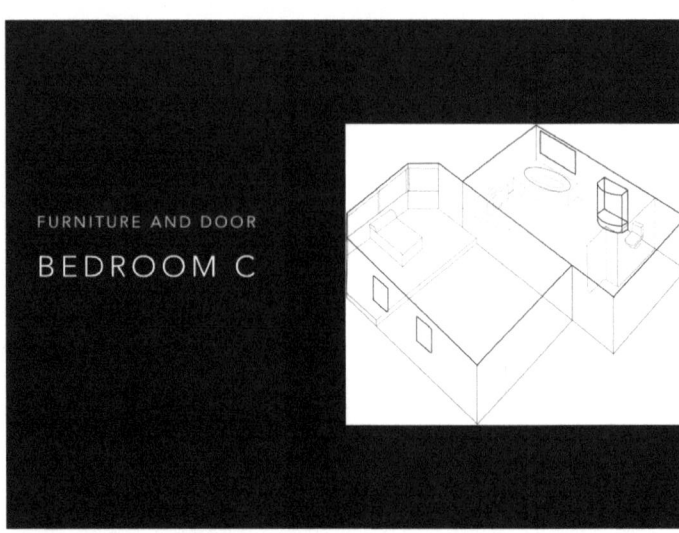

BEDROOM C

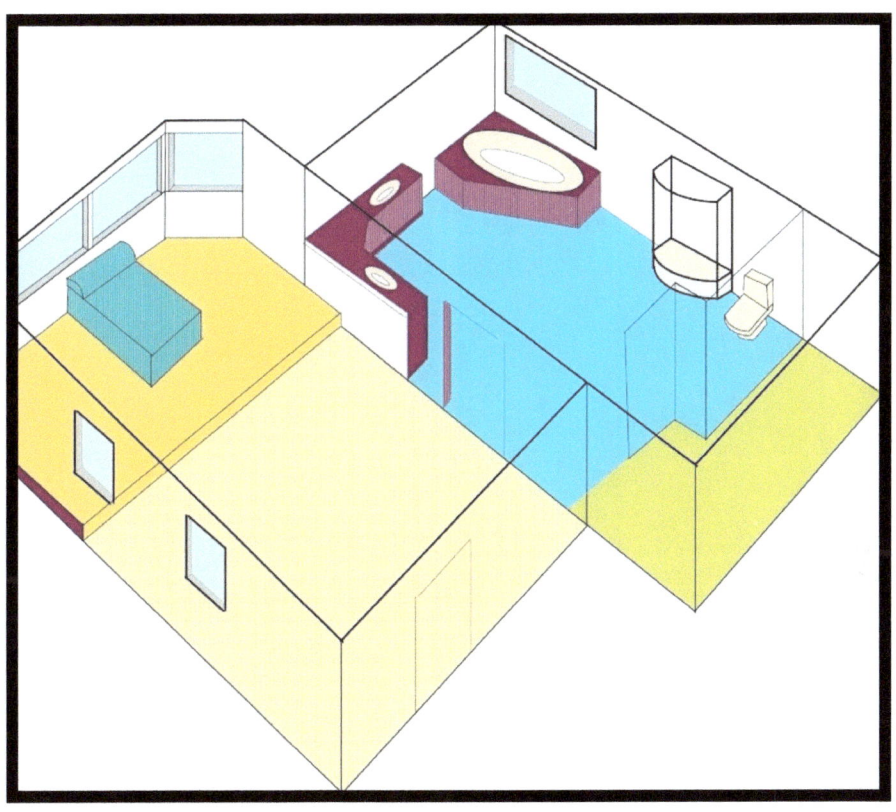

SUPPORT

Thank you for purchasing this latest version of our mini guide.

We want you to enjoy this publication and learn from it,

To this end we offer TOTAL SUPPORT - if you feel you need help or clarification on any points or receive an exercise to complete and submit, please log in to our website at

www.kbb2000.com

SURVEYING TECHNIQUES	EXTERIOR PRESENTATIONS
GRANNY FLATS	CLOAK ROOMS DRESSING ROOMS CLOSETS
KITCHEN WORKING TRIANGLE 2016	*DOUBLE WORKING TRIANGLE*
CREATIVE INTERIOR DESIGN USING A COMPUTER	CAD VS BRAIN

Avery C32016

KITCHEN PLANNING ESSENTIALS	I POINT PERSPECTIVE & VANISHING POINT
KITCHEN PLANNING APPLIANCES ESSENTIALS	2 POINT PERSPECTIVE & VANISHING POINT
KITCHEN PLANING + DESIGN	BIRDS EYE PERSPECTIVE
BATHROOM PLANNING	BEDROOM PRESENTATION
BATHROOM DESIGN	BATHROOM PRESENTATION

Avery C32011

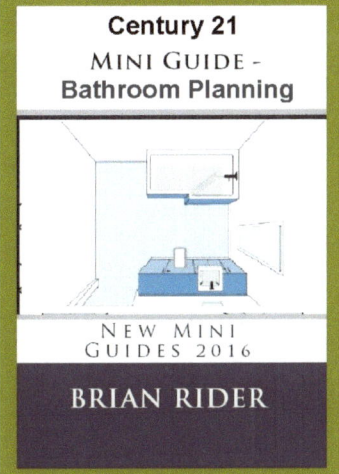

Century 21
MINI GUIDE -
Closets -Dressing Rooms

NEW MINI GUIDES 2016

BRIAN RIDER

Century 21
MINI GUIDE -
Bathroom Planning

NEW MINI GUIDES 2016

BRIAN RIDER

www.ingramcontent.com/pod-product-compliance
Lightning Source LLC
Chambersburg PA
CBHW050826290526
45792CB00001B/276